Whatever the weather

SNOW

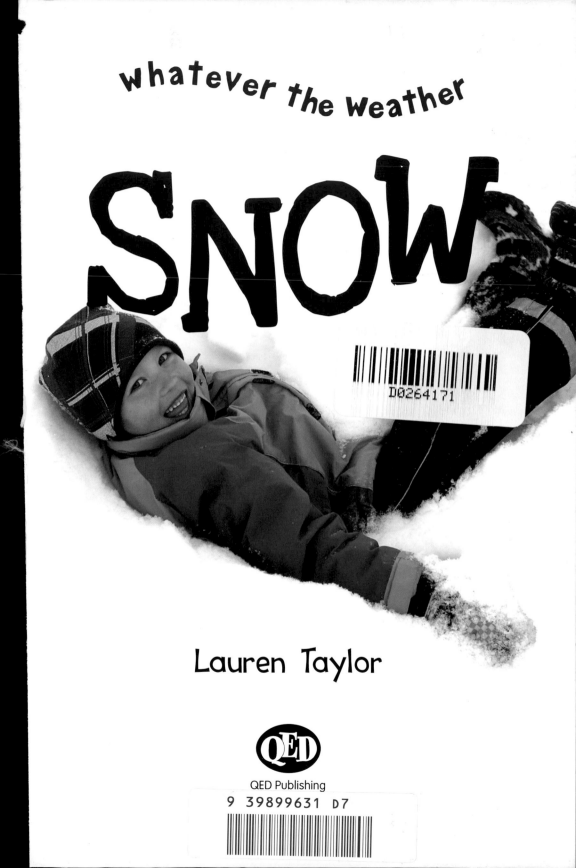

Lauren Taylor

QED

QED Publishing

9 39899631 D7

Editor: Alexandra Koken
Designer: Melissa Alaverdy
Educational consultants:
    Jillian Harker and
    Heather Adamson

Copyright © QED Publishing 2013

First published in the UK in 2013
by QED Publishing
A Quarto Group Company
230 City Road,
London EC1V 2TT

www.qed-publishing.co.uk

ISBN 978 1 78171 221 4

A catalogue record
for this book is
available from
the British Library

Printed in China

Picture credits
(t=top, b=bottom, l=left, r=right,
c=centre, fc=front cover)

Dreamstime; front cover Things
of Nature; 5c Photofl orenzo; 6
Thingsofnature; 7t Bahaberra;
7b Iofoto; 8-9 9b Dim154; 12
Viperagp; 13t Chasbrutlag, 13b;
Bellevue; 15r Dpsmedia9; 16-17
16c Vsykoczilova, 17 Nik-niklz;
18b Iperl; 21t Picsfi ve; 22-23 22b
Pfong 001 23b Maryp 23C Intst
Corbis; 10 Ocean
Getty; 14-15 14b Tim Shepard
Oxford Scientifi c Films; 15t Sven-
Erik Audt
Photoshot; 14-15 14c Ernie James
Shutterstock; 2-3 SMIT; 4 Kotenko-
Oleksandr; 5t Max Topchii; 5b
KERVELLA Rafy; 8-9, 9t Kotenko
Oleksandr; 11tr Kichigin, 11tl
Kichigin, 11cl Kichigin, 11cr
Kichigin, 11b Vadimone; 18t
Bokica; 19t Dominik Michalek;
19b Gorilla; 20-21 20b Dmitriy
Shironosov; Glossary Mat
Hayward

Words in **bold**
can be found in
the Glossary on
page 24.

Contents

What is snow?

Snow falls from the **clouds**.

It is white, wet and cold.

Sometimes snow sticks to the ground. Then, everything looks white.

When does it snow?

It snows when it is cold in winter.

In winter, many plants do not have flowers. Most of the trees have lost their leaves.

Where does snow come from?

When it is cold enough, water droplets in the clouds will **freeze**. They form small flakes of ice.

These fall as snowflakes.

Snowflakes

Up close, **snowflakes** are pretty.

They have six points.
Snowflakes also have
different patterns.

Cold as ice

Water freezes when it is cold.

Sometimes water drips off a branch or roof. If the drop freezes before it falls, it is an **icicle**.

Winter hibernation

Some animals **hibernate** in winter. When it is cold, there is not much food.

Animals sleep
for a while in
a warm place.
They wake
up in spring.

Cold all year

Some parts of the
world stay covered in
snow and ice all year.

Polar bears live in the **Arctic**. They have fur and fat to keep them warm.

Mountain snow

Some **mountain** tops are so high they stay cool. Snow covers them even in summer.

Many people like skiing and climbing on mountains.

What to wear

Always wear warm

clothes to play

in the snow.

A coat, scarf,
hat and gloves
will keep you warm.

Fun in the snow

Snow can be lots of fun. If you live near a hill, you can go tobogganing. You can also build a snowman.

Or throw
snowballs!

Glossary

Arctic   the cold area around the North Pole

cloud   a group of water droplets in the air

freeze   to become cold enough to become solid or turn to ice

hibernate   to sleep for the whole winter

icicle   an ice formation caused by water that freezes as it drips

mountain   a very large and high hill

snowflake   a single flake of snow that often has six points